Editors: Penny Scott and Ava Teherani
Graphic Design and Illustrations: Theodore Wright, IV
ISBN: 978-0-9907199-8-4
Library of Congress Control Number: 2008908105

Knowledge Power Books
A Division of Knowledge Power Communications, Inc.
www.KnowledgePowerBooks.com

Printed in the United States of America

This book is dedicated to
James "Jim" Flournoy
1915 – 2009
A Los Angeles Lawyer
He was always eager to help young lawyers.

Faith Bishop
She was my little motivator who kept pushing me
to publish this book. Whenever I wanted to move it
to the back burner to work on something I thought
more pressing, I remembered Faith's words,
"It's about time."
Thank you, Faith!

&

"King" Miles Isaiah Robinson
Our first grandson

Hello young people,

My name is Mrs. Stella L. Owens-Murrell.

I am a retired law judge.

It's exciting that you want to be a lawyer when you grow up.

At the age of 12, I decided to become a lawyer.
I was inspired by Constance Baker Motley.

Do you know who she is?

Ms. Baker Motley was the first black woman to be
appointed to the Federal Court as a Judge.

My family didn't have much money. We lived in a low-income housing project in New York. My mother encouraged me to be a lawyer, while my father thought I should be a teacher.

When I was in high school, I was a good student and worked very hard. I kept my mind on what I needed to do to get into college and then Law School.

Boys and girls, if you want to be a lawyer, you can do it! I am the only lawyer in my family and my family is very proud of me. I was told by my high school counselor that I didn't have the ability to be a lawyer.

Please remember to always follow your dreams, because my counselor was wrong. I have been an attorney for many years and just recently I retired from being a judge.

I loved being a lawyer and working as a judge. I loved being a lawyer because I was able to make a difference and people's lives were changed by my actions.

Now that I'm retired, I like to work in my community, my garden and reading a good book. I have always helped my church with their legal matters.

To be a lawyer, you will need to study, study, and study. You will need to make the best grades possible.

Law School is not for everyone. Everyone who gets a law degree may not be a lawyer. A law degree may give you many choices and open doors to many other jobs.

So you will be a lawyer when you grow up?
WOW!
My name is Saskia Asamura. I became a lawyer more than 20 years ago. My job allows me to help people and find answers to their problems, that's why I love it!

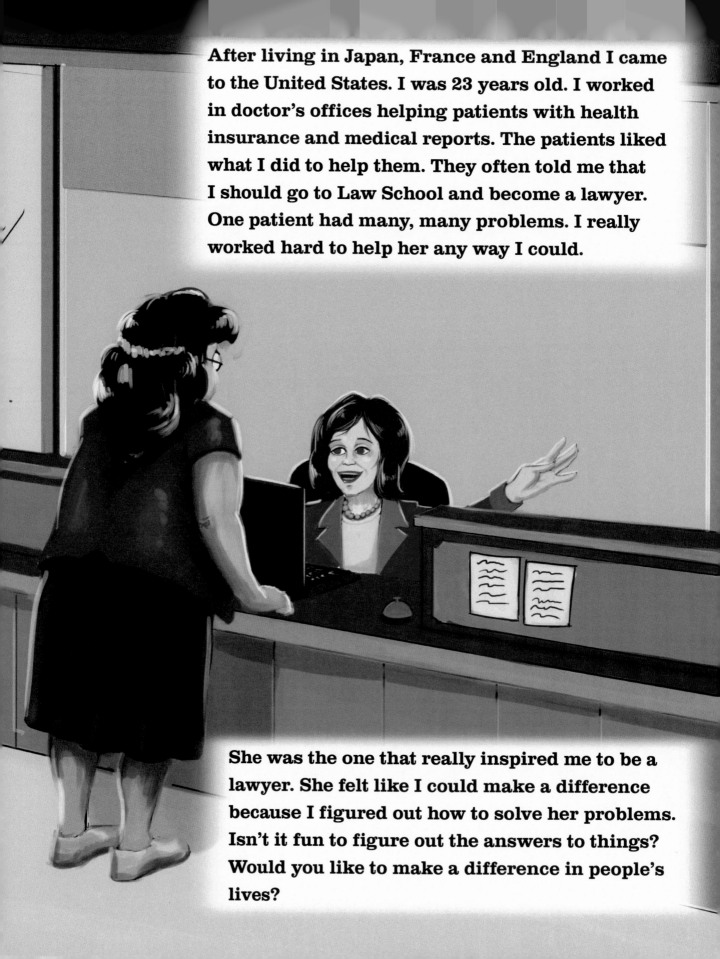

After living in Japan, France and England I came to the United States. I was 23 years old. I worked in doctor's offices helping patients with health insurance and medical reports. The patients liked what I did to help them. They often told me that I should go to Law School and become a lawyer. One patient had many, many problems. I really worked hard to help her any way I could.

She was the one that really inspired me to be a lawyer. She felt like I could make a difference because I figured out how to solve her problems. Isn't it fun to figure out the answers to things? Would you like to make a difference in people's lives?

As a little girl I always wanted to be a writer or a social worker. I started Law School when I was 31 years old. It was scary because I had to stop working to go to Law School and it cost a lot of money.

But I did it!
And you know what? I became a writer after all. As a lawyer I have to do a lot of writing. I love being a lawyer because I meet so many different and wonderful people.

My day as a lawyer is mostly writing, reading, thinking and talking. I do my best to serve my clients. I represent them in lawsuits in court. I also plan actions that will help them achieve their goals.

When I'm not working, I like having dinner with my friends. Sometimes I just like hanging out with them. At home, I like to read, work on my house, walk, and listen to music.

I also love playing with my cats.

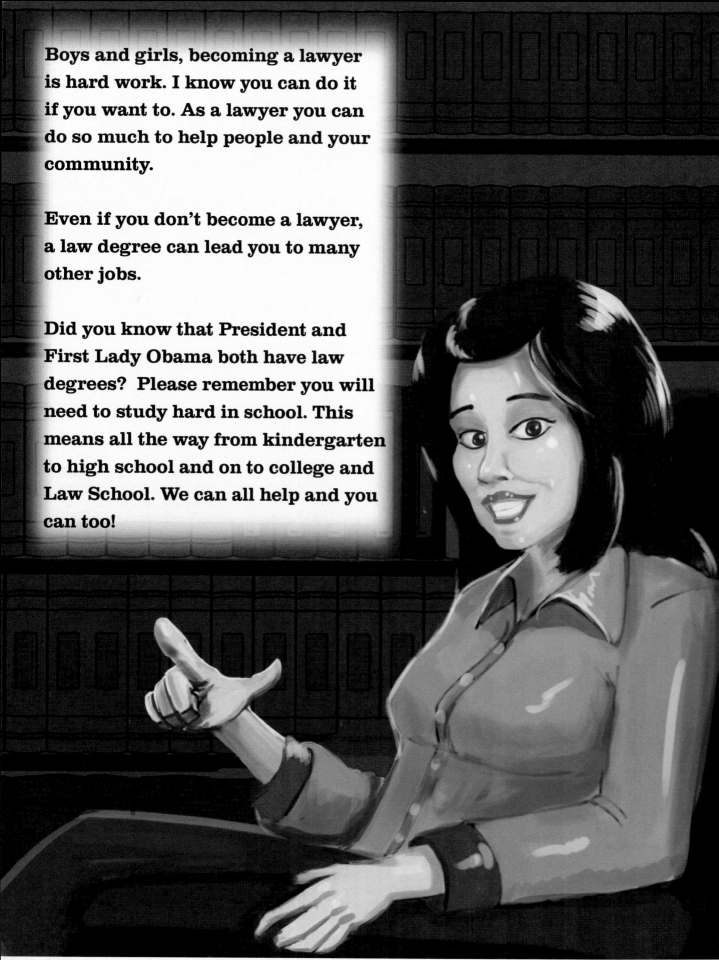

Boys and girls, becoming a lawyer is hard work. I know you can do it if you want to. As a lawyer you can do so much to help people and your community.

Even if you don't become a lawyer, a law degree can lead you to many other jobs.

Did you know that President and First Lady Obama both have law degrees? Please remember you will need to study hard in school. This means all the way from kindergarten to high school and on to college and Law School. We can all help and you can too!

Hi boys and girls!

My name is
Victor Manuel Marquez.

I'm a lawyer and my law office
is in San Francisco, California.

I think you guys are really
smart to decide now what you
will be when you grow up.

We need more good lawyers.

I decided to become a lawyer while I was in high school. During high school I got to meet Mayor Tom Bradley. He was a lawyer who became mayor of Los Angeles when I was growing up.

Mayor Bradley was a great man, and it was he who inspired me to become a lawyer.

Do you know the mayor of your city? Was he or she a lawyer before becoming mayor?

Some people told me that there were already too many lawyers. But boys and girls, I had a good feeling, and no matter what those people said, I believed there was room for one more good lawyer who wanted to do good and help people.

The reason I wanted to be a lawyer is because there were many problems in my community and I wanted to help others.

When I was growing up, there were a lot of problems in my neighborhood, but I stayed away from trouble. I stayed in high school and became involved with our student government. I was voted student body president of Venice High School in Los Angeles. I loved the responsibility and it was a great experience.

My grades in high school weren't as good as they could have been. I went to community college to improve my grades. My grades improved because I made the time to do my homework. Homework teaches you many new things, and that's really fun. I hope you like doing your homework. Do you? Doing your homework will make you smarter!

With good grades, I went to Santa Barbara University. When I graduated, I received a Community Service Award for helping other students. I was the first in my family to graduate from college. Will you be the first? Or the second? After college, I went to Santa Clara University Law School.

As a real estate lawyer, I work on the development of houses, museums, hotels, community centers, and stores.

I like to work with projects that give back to the community.

When I am not working, I love to travel. I have been to many countries like Mexico, Italy, France, China, Japan, Russia, Australia, South Africa, Zimbawe, and more. I have climbed many mountains around the world.

What countries will you visit?

I have been a lawyer for 24 years and I love it. You will love being a lawyer, too.

As a way to give back to the community, I have served as the National President of the Hispanic National Bar Association located in Washington, D.C. and I am the General Counsel to the Mexican Museum in San Francisco.

Future lawyers of America, I came to the United States from a small mining town in Mexico and I did not speak English, but I quickly learned. If I can become a good lawyer, so can you.
Just do it!

We need one more good lawyer – let that future lawyer be YOU!

Hello future lawyers!
Being a lawyer is a wonderful career. It's great that you're thinking about your future career now. That's really smart!

My name is Loretta Salzano. I have been a lawyer for 26 years, and I love it! I was inspired to be a lawyer by watching an old TV Court Show called, "Perry Mason."

Throughout my childhood, I was a good student and very focused. When I was in the 9th grade, I knew I wanted to be a lawyer. My parents and teachers supported my decision.
Are you a good student?

Boys and girls to be a lawyer, you must:

1. Graduate from High School
2. Graduate from College
3. Graduate from Law School
4. Make excellent grades along the way
5. Pass a State Bar Examination

Now, I know this looks like a lot to accomplish, and it is, but I know you can do it, right?

Lawyers are extremely determined and disciplined.

During college and Law School, I studied and worked very hard.

I practiced time management.

Not only did I complete my assignments, but I had fun, too!

As I said, I was a good student in classes like English and sociology. But in classes involving numbers (math, algebra, trigonometry, etc.), I was a disaster! I had problems learning math concepts. Even when I was really struggling, I didn't give up. I was determined and asked for help. Do you ask for help in difficult classes?

I was very active in high school and had a wonderful time. I started a culture club, where students learned about other cultures and the arts. I sang in the chorus, and I starred in a school play. Some of my best memories were made in high school.

In college, many classes were really hard. I stressed about how to control my workload. It was important to make good grades so I could attend an excellent Law School. After a while, I learned the ropes, and it all worked out.

Applying for Law School was stressful, too. I had to study and pass the Law School Admissions Test (LSAT) with high scores to be accepted into Law School. I graduated from the University of Michigan and attended Law School there.

I'm not the only lawyer in my family. One of my younger sisters is a lawyer, too. Our parents are very proud of us.

Will you be the first lawyer in your family?

Have you decided what college you will attend?

I love being a lawyer because I enjoy talking to groups. I teach them about the laws that affect their businesses. I really love entertaining my clients and future clients. I also love my connection in professional organizations. I have made many friends.

My day as a lawyer is very busy.

I write letters and create legal documents. I spend a lot of time on the phone helping my clients learn the law, while trying to solve their problems. When I'm not traveling on business, I take a client or future client to lunch every day.

During the time when I'm not working as a lawyer, I like to travel, eat and cook. I think my husband and 12-year old son are the best entertainment of all.

What do you like to do when you're not in school?

Future lawyers, there are many different ways to practice law.

It took me several years to find the right job as a lawyer. I suggest, when you can, talk to different lawyers and spend time with them.

Ask lots of questions. Lawyers love to talk.

One last thing, do not settle on what you think a lawyer should be. Do not settle on how a lawyer should look. Just be true to yourself and you will find the right direction and be happy in your career.

Hi Boys and Girls,
I'm delighted that you're reading this book. I wish there was a book like this when I was your age.

My name is Corlandos Scott and I have been a lawyer for 3 ½ years. Education was very important to my grandmother. She made sure I understood that education was my best chance to create a good life for me and my future family. Although, my grandmother didn't encourage me to become a lawyer or any other professional, her attitude inspired me to be in a profession that I thought was noble and well respected.

I first thought about becoming a lawyer as a 10-year old. I saw a lawyer on TV and I said to myself, "I could do that." I soon forgot about that day.

Years later, when I was a senior in college, I made my decision to apply for Law School.

In high school, I was not a very disciplined student. My grades were fair, but not because of studying.

Rather, I was able to get through high school with a basic understanding of the subjects.

Hopefully you are a disciplined student.

Before my final decision to become a lawyer, I had some obstacles. One obstacle was making sure that my entrance exam score was high enough to make-up for my low GPA. Had I made the decision to go to Law School earlier, I would have paid closer attention to my grades. A high GPA helps when applying to Law School.

My other obstacle was that I worked on a job for 5 years between college and Law School. I had to train myself with the idea of studying, attending class and test-taking.

Almost every day in college I had a challenge. My biggest challenge was creating a "system for success." Throughout high school, I simply studied when I felt I needed to study. However in college, I learned that I needed to be more disciplined. The material was new and vast, much more than it was in high school.

These challenges would not have been as difficult had I began practicing good study habits in elementary and high school. Law School also presented many challenges. The vocabulary of law was new to me, as well as the amount of reading and writing that was required.

Students, please make an effort to develop good study habits now. You will experience less challenges.

I graduated from the University of North Alabama with a Bachelor of Science in Communications. I graduated from Law School at the University of Michigan.

When I became a lawyer, my family was extremely proud. I was the first member of my family to attend college.

So, it was especially satisfying to help set a new standard for the young members of my family.

I am the first of hopefully many other lawyers in my family to come.

As a lawyer, I enjoy the feeling of helping a client solve problems. It's extremely rewarding to know that I help individuals accomplish goals or avoid pitfalls. I try to prepare for a work day as a lawyer by creating a list of priorities the day before.

When I get to work, I look at the priority list and begin at the top. Most days, I speak with clients and work on contracts. Other days, I appear in court to represent a client before a judge.

On my days off, I enjoy watching sports on TV. I like to go to movies, play basketball and golf. I also play the saxophone and sometimes I play a special song for my church.

I hope you will become a lawyer when you grow up. However, I suggest you begin sharpening your reading and reading comprehension skills.

Much of being a lawyer involves reading a law and understanding what it means. Also, understand that every area of life is affected in some way by laws. Find what else you're passionate about, whether it's sports, business, finance or something else. Then, focus your law career around that.

The earlier you begin to focus on developing good grades and reading and writing skills, the easier your journey to law will be; and be encouraged!

Even if you find yourself with less than stellar grades in school, that does not make you a failure. Your road may be challenging, however, just a little hard work will make a difference.

You can go from being a mediocre student to a graduate of one of the top 10 Law Schools in the nation!

Corlandos Scott
Attorney at Law

About the Author:

I Will Be A Lawyer When I Grow Up is the second book of the *I Will Be* empowerment book series for children.

Willa Robinson is the creator of the series and she is extremely grateful to the lawyers who shared their stories.

A special thanks to Retired Judge, Mrs. Stella Owens-Murrell, Attorney Saskia Asamura, Attorney Victor Manuel Marquez, Attorney Loretta Salzano, and Attorney Corlandos Scott.

The purpose of the *I Will Be* book series is to encourage young people to start thinking and dreaming about their future careers.

The next books to be published are *I Will Be A Nurse When I Grow Up* and *I Will Be A Doctor When I Grow Up*. Mrs. Robinson believes, "it's never too early to help children think about their futures."